The First Thanksgiving

A Play for Children

Paula Abeles

OAK LEAF
P R E S S

Oak Leaf Press
5576 Norbeck Road
Rockville, Maryland 20855

Oak Leaf Press and the portrayal of the oak leaves and acorns are registered trademarks of Oak Leaf Press, LLC.

Attention Corporations and Organizations:
Most Oak Leaf Press books are available at quantity discounts with bulk purchase for educational, business, or sales promotion use.

The First Thanksgiving
A Play For Children

ISBN: 978-0-9840314-0-5

Library of Congress Catalog Card Number: 2011942009
Cataloging-in Publication Data is on file with the Library of Congress
Children/play/historical/U.S. history/Pilgrims

Visit Oak Leaf Press on the World Wide Web at
www.oakleafpress.net

Manufactured in the United States of America
Published simultaneously in Canada

Acknowledgements

This play is based on the following works by two wonderful authors:

The Story of the Pilgrims by Katherine Ross, illustrated by Carolyn Croll and The First Thanksgiving by Linda Hayward and Illustrated by James Watling.

Other books that are great for children include:

The Pilgrims' First Thanksgiving by Ann McGovern and illustrated by Elroy Freem.

What Is Thanksgiving? by Michele Medlock Adams, illustrated by Amy Wummer.

If You Were At The First Thanksgiving by Anne Kamma and illustrated by Bert Dodson.

And for younger children-

Thanksgiving Is For Giving Thanks, by Margaret Sutherland and illustrated by Sonja Lamut.

Dedication

This play is dedicated to Winthrop and Everett (otherwise known as "The King" and "Narrator 1 /Worm Eater 1") whose family history reflects the great traditions of both the European settlers and the Native Americans from whom they are descended.

And, in gratitude to teachers like Ms. Brigid McGuire of Sequoyah Elementary School, who go above and beyond the call of duty—everyday—to motivate, inspire and inform.
Thank you all.

Authors Note:

This play has 17 speaking parts, although some parts consist of only one line. As written, the narrators are generally assigned three paragraphs each, but this could be easily adjusted to accommodate more or fewer children. There are also non-speaking 'moving parts' (like the ship and the waves, for example) for non-readers. The play relies on simple props (list included) that are readily available, or can be made easily at home or in the classroom with foam core, paint, and (a little) imagination. Resources for costumes are listed in the back.

The First Thanksgiving

1620 A. D.

Characters In Order of Appearance:

Narrator (s) ~9:
King of England~
Pilgrim Woman~
Pilgrims~ Narrators & assembled company
The Mayflower~
The Waves~
The Worm Eaters~
Corey, The dog~
Samoset~~ First Indian friend~
Squanto~~ Indian guide & instructor~
Native American Braves~
Massasoit~ The Indian King~
Native Americans~ Narrators & assembled
company

Narrator (1) –:

In 1609, in the country known as England, there lived a small group of people called Pilgrims. The Pilgrims did not want to participate in the English national church. They wanted to worship God in their own way, in their own church. But under the King's law, this was not allowed. So the Pilgrims were forced to meet each other and say their prayers in secret.

When the King found out that the Pilgrim's were disobeying the law, he was very angry. Many of their leaders were arrested and imprisoned. The other Pilgrims realized it was too dangerous for them to stay in England, and they went to Holland where they were allowed to practice their religion.

But the Pilgrims were not happy in Holland. They missed the language and traditions of their native country.

So, the Pilgrims decided to sail to America. The English King was glad to see them go. He was tired of them causing problems in his kingdom.

King of England-
(Pointing to huddled Pilgrims) " Go away and stay away! Good riddance..."

Narrator (2)- :

The Pilgrims packed up what belongings they could carry and said a tearful goodbye to their homes and their friends, and the world they knew. On a mild day in autumn, forty-four Pilgrims set sail for a new world called America, which was across the wide ocean. But it wasn't only Pilgrims who sailed on the Mayflower.

Sixty-six other people-- who hoped for land and adventure-- came too. Together, they hoped to find more freedom and a better life.

But they knew their life would not be an easy one. Because none of the passengers could afford the cost of their passage and their supplies, they were all bound to work for seven years for a group of English investors.

(Pilgrims, kissing and hugging their friends):

Pilgrim Woman-
"Goodbye. Keep us in your prayers! We'll miss you! Bye-Bye!"

Narrator (2)-:
One hundred and twenty passengers crowded onto the small wooden ship. The Mayflower was on its way! But halfway across the great

Atlantic Ocean, the Mayflower was hit by terrible storms.

(Cardboard ship buffeted by "jumping" cardboard waves)

Narrator (3)~:

For many weeks the storms raged on, and enormous waves crested and rolled across the ship's deck. To many of the passengers, it seemed as if the wooden ship had little chance against the fury of the ocean.

Worse still, the water was too rough to catch fresh fish. The Pilgrims were forced to rely on the stores of food they had brought with them: sour pickled beef, moldy cheese and hard stale bread.

Because it was hard to preserve food, most of the bread that remained was crawling with worms. The Pilgrims and the other passengers were hungry and miserable.

(Pilgrims eating bread, throw it to the ground):

Pilgrim Men-
"Yeeech...... worms!"

Narrator (4)-:

After sixty-five days at sea, on November 10, 1620, the Pilgrims heard the words they had been praying for:

Voice (offstage): "Land-ho"

Narrator (4)-:

After many days of exploring up and down the coast, the Pilgrims at last found a deep harbor near good farmland. Here they would make their home. The Pilgrims named it Plymouth in honor of the port in England from which they had sailed..

But the new settlers were fearful of the strange people who lived on these tree-lined shores. They had heard stories that the native people whom they called 'indians' were wild and dangerous. So, while some stood guard against attack by Indians or wild animals, the other settlers began to build houses.

As each day grew a little colder and a little darker, they tried to work as quickly as they could. Winter was coming!

(Pilgrim girls walk to and fro with baskets. Pilgrim boys carry pieces of cardboard "lumber" and work with "tools". Everyone looks busy. Sound of hammering heard offstage)

Narrator (5)-:

And a terrible winter it was! There were dark days of bleak and bitter cold— far colder than any they had known back in England. Snow and sleet and high winds battered the Pilgrim's little houses. The Pilgrims huddled together for warmth, but there was hardly enough to eat. Almost everyone got sick.

(Pilgrims huddle for warmth, much coughing and sneezing).

Narrator (5)~:

Many people died...

(Pilgrims fall over dead, stick out their tongues).

Narrator (6)~:

By the end of winter—only 50-- less than half-- of the Pilgrims were still alive. The long, sad winter passed and spring arrived. Indians were sighted nearby. They came closer and closer. The Pilgrims were very afraid. With so few people, the Pilgrims knew that if the Indians attacked, they would not be able to defend themselves.

Then one day, a Native American walked right into the settlement! The children were terrified....

(Pilgrims huddle together looking terrified as an Indian approaches....dog barks)

Corey, the NewFoundland dog:
"Woof. Woof"

Narrator (6)~:

...but the Abnaki tribe member named Samoset smiled and said in English:

Samoset- (raising his palm in the "how" gesture):
"Welcome"

Narrator (6)~:

Soon other Native Americans came to visit the settlement. The Pilgrims were delighted to find friends that were willing to help them survive in this new, wild land.

Squanto:
"My name is Squanto. So that you may eat, I will show your men where to catch fish and hunt animals. So that you will be well, I will show your women how to find nuts and berries and wild herbs in the forest. And, so that there will be peace between us for generations, I will show your children how to plant corn, in the way

of my people, so that the soil will be rich, and the corn will grow."

(Squanto takes a fish and shows a group of interested pilgrims how to dig a hole, place the fish and the corn kernels in the hole and cover it up).

Narrator (7) ~:

Squanto and the other Native Americans taught their Pilgrim friends well. They taught them how to tap maple trees for sap. They showed them which plants were poisonous, and which could be used for medicine. They taught them how to cure meats over a smoke fire. In the spring, they helped them plant seeds in the rich soil. With great care, the Pilgrims watched their crops grow and prosper. When autumn came, the Pilgrims rejoiced over their bountiful harvest--- bright ears of sweet corn, fat pumpkins, peas, beans and yellow squash, and lots of fragrant green herbs.

The Pilgrims were very thankful! Not only would they be able to store enough food to last them through the winter ahead, but the native people they had so feared, had become their great friends. The Pilgrims knew they could never have survived without the Native Americans.

To show their appreciation, the Pilgrims decided to invite the Native Americans to a feast of 'thanksgiving' to celebrate their successful harvest. The Pilgrims were delighted and honored to learn that even the King of the Patuxet tribe, Massasoit (mass-uh-SO-it) was planning to come. But when the great day came, and Massasoit arrived, the Pilgrims were shocked to see he had brought <u>ninety</u> members of his tribe with him!

(Pilgrims standing around with baskets of food, look worried as Indians approach)

Narrator (8)-:

The Pilgrims were embarrassed and worried. They did not want to offend the Native Americans or King Massasoit, who had been so generous with them. But, they had hoped the food they had harvested would last them through the coming winter. Even if they used up all their stores, how could they feed so many people?

But Massasoit was very wise. He sensed the uneasiness of his new friends, and he wanted to spare them the shame they would feel if there was not enough food for their honored guests. So, he quickly gave an order to the young men from his tribe:

Massasoit:
"Young braves: Go now into the forest and bring enough deer to feed us all."

(Braves return- laden with deer and skins)

Narrator (8)~:

Soon the young braves, who were skillful hunters, returned with five deer. Now, there was enough food for everyone!

Massasoit- (to the Braves):
"In celebration of your great skill and thanks giving for your great success, let us now dance in the tradition of our fathers."

(Indian braves dance to accompaniment of drums)

Narrator (9)~:

For three days and nights, The Pilgrims and the Native Americans ate and drank and danced. The Native American and Pilgrim children played games together. Everyone had a wonderful time. On the last day, the Native Americans and the Pilgrims signed a treaty promising to help each other and be at peace. The treaty was kept for fifty-four years.

For many years the custom of celebrating Thanksgiving continued. During the American Revolution, the Continental Congress suggested making it a national holiday, but nothing happened for many years. In 1817, New York State made the holiday official for New York residents, and many other states followed suit. Finally, in 1863, Thanksgiving became a national holiday for everyone.

As we gather with our friends and family over a plentiful repast, we remember the sacrifices of the Pilgrims and the kindness and generosity of their friends and teachers, the Native American Indians.

The End.

SONG

If you wish to close your production with a song, this is a traditional Thanksgiving song that was very popular in the 17th century. It is also a Thanksgiving play classic!

"WE GATHER TOGETHER"

Text: Nederlandtsch Gedercklanck. Translated by Theodore Baker
Music 16th century Dutch melody arranged by Edward Krenser (1838-1914)
For sheet music: http://www.makingmusicfun.net/pdf/sheet_music/we-gather-together-piano.pdf

1   We gather together
to ask the Lord's blessing;
he chastens and hastens
his will to make known.
The wicked oppressing
now cease from distressing.
Sing praises to his name,
he forgets not his own.

2.   Beside us to guide us,
our God with us joining,
ordaining, maintaining
his kingdom divine;
so from the beginning
the fight we were winning;
thou, Lord, wast at our side,
all glory be thine!

3.   We all do extol thee,
thou leader triumphant,
and pray that thou still
our defender wilt be.
Let thy congregation
escape tribulation;
thy name be ever praised!
O Lord, make us free

PROPS REQUIRED:

Throne chair for King
Cardboard ship cut-out
Waves cardboard cut-outs
Animal furs (for deer) on wooden pole/branch
Vegetables
Corn
Baskets
Bread
Cardboard "lumber"   (painted foam core cut in lengths)
Wooden spoon
Drums
Real hammer for sound effects
plastic "tools"
Plastic fish

COSTUME REQUIREMENTS (By character)

Narrator (s)-9: Puritan & Native American mixed
King of England- "King" outfit, crown, cloak
Pilgrim Woman- Pilgrim costume
Pilgrims- Narrators & assembled company
The Mayflower- Ship painted on standard foam core
The Waves- waves painted on standard foam core and cut out

The Worm Eaters- Puritan costumes

Corey, The dog- Dog costume

Samoset-- First Indian friend- Native American costume

Squanto-- Indian guide & instructor- Native American costume

Native American Braves- Native American costume

Massasoit- The Indian King- Native American costume-Chief Headdress

Native Americans- Narrators & assembled company

If you don't plan to purchase costumes, but are going to try to assemble them from clothes or costumes on-hand—here are the basics:

<u>Pilgrim Girl Costume:</u>

Grey or Black long dress (with long sleeves) or separates

White apron

White cotton bonnet

Black shoes

Accessories: basket, copper kettle or pot

<u>Pilgrim Boy Costume</u>

White long sleeved shirt

Black or brown pants (rolled up just below knee)

Long white socks or stockings

Black or brown shoes

Accessories: Straw hat, axe

Native American (boy or girl)
Brown pants and top (or dress for girl)
Headband with feather, braids
Spear, bow & arrow, wooden bowl

RESOURCES FOR COSTUMES:

Although there may still be companies that rent costumes in your local area, it is generally just as economical to buy as to rent. In addition to the companies listed below, you can frequently find great costumes and accessories on ebay (www.ebay.com).

Depending on your budget, many of these companies also stock some fun props that the kids will enjoy adding to their costumes (Examples: peace pipe, raccoon hat, bow & arrow, colonial shoe buckles etc.). Search by Holiday/Thanksgiving or "Colonial", "Pilgrim", "Indian", "Native American". Most costumes range in price from about $15~$25. See examples at the end.

Costume Express/Buy Costumes.com

16205 West Small Road
New Berlin, WI 53151
800-459-2969
www.costumeexpress.com;
www.buycostumes.com

Costume Craze
350 West Center Street
Pleasant Grove, UT 84062
888-922-7293
www.costumecraze.com

Wholesale Halloween Costumes
402 Main Street, Suite 100-192
Metuchen, NJ 08840
855-268-8008
www.wholesalehalloweencostumes.com

Costume Hub
8250 Northeast Underground Drive
Pillar 156-G
Kansas City, MO 64161
800-899-5540
www.costumehub.com

Costume Supercenter
45 Fernwood Avenue
Edison, New Jersey 08837
888-575-5575
www.costumesupercenter.com

Costumes4Less.com
7625 East Rosecrans Avenue, #3
Paramount, CA 90723
888-224-7973
www.costumes4less.com

Costume Notes:

Stage Notes:

_____

_____

_____

_____

_____

_____

_____

_____

_____

_____

_____

Stage Notes:

Stage Notes:

www.ingramcontent.com/pod-product-compliance
Lightning Source LLC
Chambersburg PA
CBHW080536030426
42337CB00023B/4767